Aural Book 2

Specimen Aural Tests

for Trinity College London exams from 2017

Grades 6-8

Published by
Trinity College London Press
trinitycollege.com

Registered in England
Company no. 09726123

Copyright © 2016 Trinity College London Press
Second impression, June 2017

Printed in England by Caligraving Ltd.

Contents

Acknowledgements

Trinity College London Press gratefully acknowledges the contribution of David Gaukroger and Chris Lawry, who composed the musical examples in this book. We thank Peter Wild for performing the piano on the CD recordings, and also Luise Horrocks, for being our examiner voiceover on the CDs.

Grateful thanks are due to Tim Grant-Jones, author of the previous Aural Book 2, on which this publication is closely modelled.

In addition, thanks are extended to all the teachers, students and examiners around the world whose comments have contributed to the development of this suite of tests.

Introduction

Aural skill - the ability to listen intelligently to music and to understand what has been heard - forms a vital part of the training of musicians at all levels. The assessment of this skill in practical exams ensures that it is developed alongside instrumental or vocal ability.

This book supports the suite of aural tests developed for use in Trinity College London grade exams from 2017. This set is a development of the successful format of the previous set of tests, retaining the practice of using a single piece of music for all questions. By answering a series of questions all based on the same piece of music, candidates will find that they develop their ability to listen with perception; this process is enhanced by sections of the tests which encourage reading skills and eye-to-ear co-ordination.

The format of the tests at Grades 6-8 is similar to that of the previous set, although the structure and scope of the answers expected from candidates is more clearly defined. In place of the open-ended discussion of features in the previous set, candidates now comment on a specific number of features: time signature, dynamics and articulation in Question 1, and a further two or three characteristics (depending on grade) in Question 2.

Using this book:

This book is designed to be used effectively either by teachers during lessons or by candidates themselves at home. As teachers will generally wish to supply their own explanations of the questions, the text is addressed primarily to the candidate.

For each grade the following information is given:

About the test piece – gives the parameters of the test piece, so that candidates understand the features of the piece, and so that teachers may devise further sample tests if they wish.

What the examiner will do – explains how the examiner will run the test, so that candidates can feel at ease in the exam and so that teachers can run the tests in the same way.

What you will be asked to do – explains what the candidate will be asked to do for each question, so that candidates and teachers clearly understand what the task involves.

What the question is for – explains the musical reasons for the question, enabling candidates and teachers to understand the skills being developed and assessed.

Hints – useful tips on how to prepare for and succeed at each test, covering both valuable musical knowledge and practical hints for the exam itself.

Information for teachers – an overview of the rationale for each section of the tests, highlighting the progression of each skill through the grades and giving tips for adapting the tests to ask a wider selection of questions.

At the end of each grade candidates are invited to try the sample tests, either by using the CD or with their teacher playing the questions.

The **Answer Booklet** contains the text and printed music from the CDs so that teachers can play the examples to their pupils.

Each example is also annotated with answers clearly indicated, so that candidates can be assisted in their preparation by parents or friends with limited (or no) musical knowledge.

The examples use a variety of styles and are suitable for a range of pianistic abilities. They are not exhaustive, but give ample practice material, while the parameters of the test piece are given at each grade to enable teachers to select suitable supplementary material if necessary.

Using the CDs:

Each track contains a complete set of questions including spoken text and music. The text and music for the CDs may be found in the Answer Booklet, along with answers to the questions.

Tips for preparing for the aural tests

- The questions for Grades 6-8 cover many aspects of music, including:
  - metre
  - phrasing
  - style
  - dynamics
  - articulation
  - rhythm
  - texture
  - tonality
- You can practise the majority of the aural tests with most types of music, including pieces you play or sing and those you listen to, so you can start to prepare for your exam well in advance.
- Find out the title of each piece of music you listen to or play. You should look for the name of the composer, artist or band who created it, as well as seeing when it was written. Knowing the date will help you identify the different styles of music, for example Baroque in the 17th and early 18th centuries, or jazz and rock in the 20th and 21st.
- Try to listen to music in an active way. Don't just hear the sound that the music makes, but ask yourself questions about what is going on. It can be useful to concentrate on just one aspect at a time. Here are some other questions you could ask about the music you listen to:
  - are there any elements of the music's style that you have heard before?
  - is the composer one that you know? How is this piece like other works of theirs?
  - is the texture thick or thin?
  - what feeling (if any) does the music express?
  - what instruments are playing? Are they acoustic or electronic?
  - does the harmony do what you would expect or is it full of surprises?
  - can you hear recognisable chords? Are there cadences?
- As you can see, there are many, many questions you can ask about any piece of music you hear. You will not spot everything in one hearing, and there is no reason why you should! Music can take a very long time to create, and this can be because the composer is putting so much into the piece. It is no surprise, therefore, that it can take listeners a long time to work their way through all the different layers.

Grade 6

About the test piece:

metre	$\frac{2}{4}$, $\frac{3}{4}$, $\frac{4}{4}$ or $\frac{6}{8}$
length	8 bars
key	major
style	piano style using treble and bass clefs
features	contains a modulation to the subdominant, dominant or relative minor

All questions will be based on the same piece of music.

Question 1

What the examiner will do:

Play the piece twice.

What you will be asked to do:

i)   Tell the examiner the **time signature.**
ii) Tell the examiner about the **dynamics.**
iii) Tell the examiner about the **articulation.**

What the question is for:

▶   To learn to recognise the **time signature** of a piece.
▶   To develop your skills in recognising **how the music was played.**
▶   To learn the **words** to describe what you hear.

Hints

Time signature

▶   Tapping or clapping the rhythm and stressing the strong beats while you listen is perhaps the easiest and most effective way to work out the time signature.

▶   Don't forget that the time might be simple (where the beat is easily divisible by 2) or compound (where the beat is easily divisible by 3).

▶   All of the time signatures for this grade appeared in earlier grades, so you might find it useful to refer to Aural Book 1 which includes more information about time signatures and hints on recognising them.

Hints

Dynamics

▶ Dynamic changes add interest to music, and the test piece will contain a number of variations of dynamic. Listen first for the overall dynamic plan from phrase to phrase. Then listen for rising and falling within phrases, echo effects and other contrasts.

▶ Learn the words to describe different dynamics, as well as the terms used to express gradual dynamic changes (for example *crescendo* and *diminuendo*).

Articulation

▶ The piece may use a mixture of *staccato* and *legato* notes, as well as accents.

▶ Explain how the articulation is used, referring to any distinctive features of the piece.

Question 2

What the examiner will do:

Play the piece twice.

What you will be asked to do:

Tell the examiner about two other characteristics of the piece.

What the question is for:

▶ To develop your skills in **recognising the styles of pieces of music**, and the **compositional devices** they feature.

▶ To develop your skills in **recognising how the music was played.**

▶ To learn the **words** to describe what you hear.

Hints

This question gives you an opportunity to describe what you hear. There are many characteristics of each piece which could be identified here, although you should avoid any references to features already discussed (time signature, dynamics and articulation). You might like to consider the following:

Style

▶ The style of the music is like the style of food a restaurant serves; there can be many different dishes but they may all be the same style: Italian, Greek, Chinese, etc. The main features of the music all go to make up the style. To determine this, listen to features such as the shape of the melody, harmony, how the dynamics and other expressive detail are used, how the different sections of the music relate to each other, and so on. All of these give clues to the style of the music.

▶ Certain characteristics might lead you to suggest:
  – a particular period of music in which it might have been written (eg. Baroque, Classical, etc)
  – a particular style or dance form that the music represents (eg. march, waltz).

▶ Listening to and playing a wide range of pieces is the best way to learn to identify different musical styles.

Texture

▶ Texture describes how the musical lines work together. Make sure you know how to describe texture as:
  – monophonic (a single line, no harmony or accompaniment)
  – homophonic (all sounds moving with the same rhythm)
  – polyphonic (several musical ideas moving independently)

▶ There are other ways of explaining texture, such as:
  – unison or octaves
  – 2-part, 3-part, 4-part
  – imitative

▶ As the piece will be played on the piano, you might notice common piano figurations such as:
  – waltz-style accompaniment ('oom cha cha')
  – march-style accompaniment ('oom pah')
  – melody in the bass, or in the middle of the texture
  – Alberti bass

▶ The texture might also be sparse or dense, and may be concentrated in the treble or the bass.

Compositional devices

▶ Listen for compositional devices such as sequences, pedal notes, chromatic passages and/or notes, dotted rhythms, cadences, passing notes, repetition, imitation, syncopation, ornamentation and anacrusis.

▶ In some cases these will be typical features of the style or period – for example ornamentation and decorated cadences in Baroque pieces, or swung quavers and syncopation in jazz pieces.

Question 3

What the examiner will do:
- State the opening key of the piece and play the key-chord.
- Play the first four bars of the piece once.

What you will be asked to do:
Tell the examiner into which key the music has modulated: the subdominant, dominant or relative minor.

What the question is for:
- To develop your skills in **recognising key changes (modulations)**.
- To learn the **words** to describe what you hear.

Hints
- **Learn the circle of 5ths** for major keys. By now, you will probably have played (or sung) music and scales & arpeggios in most of these keys.
- Your answer may be given as either the key or the technical name – for example in C major: 'to G major' or 'to the dominant'.
- If you want to state the actual modulated key, think of the possible modulated keys as soon as you are told the key of the piece. For example, a piece in C major could modulate to F major (the subdominant), G major (the dominant) or A minor (the relative minor).
- A modulation to the dominant feels as if something bright and exciting has happened.
- A modulation to the subdominant involves the act of flattening one of the notes, which can make the effect of the modulation feel less assertive.
- The test piece is in a major key, so if it modulates to a minor key, it will be to the relative minor. Dominant keys and subdominant keys will both be major.
- Try holding the tonic note in your head. If the modulation is to the subdominant or the relative minor the original tonic note will still fit with the tonic chord of the new key. If the original tonic note clashes with the new tonic chord then the piece has modulated to the dominant.

The circle of 5ths

▶ The dominant key is the next key to the tonic following the circle clockwise (adding a sharp to, or removing a flat from, the key signature).

▶ The subdominant is the next key to the tonic following the circle anticlockwise (removing a sharp from, or adding a flat to, the key signature).

▶ The relative minor is the minor key that shares the key signature of the tonic.

▶ The diagram shows the tonic, dominant and subdominant keys starting with C major.

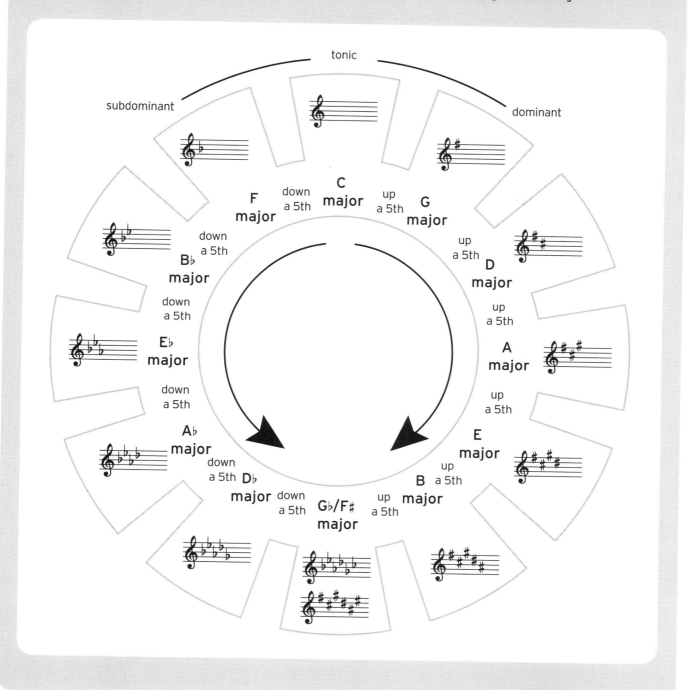

Question 4

What the examiner will do:

▶ Give you a printed copy of the piece.

▶ Play the piece twice in a version with two changes to the melody line. The changes may be to the pitch or to the rhythm or both.

What you will be asked to do:

Identify where the changes were, and whether they were to the pitch or rhythm.

What the question is for:

▶ To develop your **musical memory**.

▶ To develop your **awareness of pitch and rhythm**.

▶ To develop your skills in **relating the music you see to what you hear**.

▶ To improve the **accuracy of your reading**.

Hints

▶ You will already have heard the complete original version **four times** before hearing the changed version.

▶ Remember that at this grade **both changes will appear in the melody line**.

▶ Try to concentrate on listening to the melody while you are following the printed music.

▶ Concentrate on the shape of the melody and look out for the places where what you hear does not match what you are looking at.

▶ Either use the printed copy to point to the bar in which each change occurred, or tell the examiner the bar numbers where the changes occurred.

▶ You do not have to describe the changes; you only need to identify where they occurred and state whether they were to the pitch or to the rhythm.

▶ Remember that **you are not allowed to make any marks on the copy of the music** you have been given, **or make any other notes during the test**. You could point your finger at the first change to help you remember where it was while you look and listen for the second change.

Try the tests

CD1 [01] – [10]   Listen to the CD or ask your teacher to play the tests on the piano for you. Each track on the CD contains a complete set of questions. Printed opposite is the music you will need for Question 4 of each set. Don't look at the music until you reach Question 4. The answers to the tests can be found on pages 4–13 of the **Answer Booklet**.

Music for Grade 6 Question 4

01   Test 1

02   Test 2

03 Test 3

04 Test 4

05 **Test 5**

06 **Test 6**

07 **Test 7**

08 **Test 8**

09 **Test 9**

10 **Test 10**

Grade 7

About the test piece:

metre	$\frac{2}{4}, \frac{3}{4}, \frac{4}{4}$ or $\frac{6}{8}$
length	8 bars
key	major or minor
style	piano style using treble and bass clefs
features	contains a modulation to the subdominant, dominant or relative key

All questions will be based on the same piece of music.

Question 1

What the examiner will do:

Play the piece twice.

What you will be asked to do:

i) Tell the examiner the **time signature.**

ii) Tell the examiner about the **dynamics.**

iii) Tell the examiner about the **articulation.**

What the question is for:

▶ To learn to recognise the **time signature** of a piece.

▶ To develop your skills in recognising **how the music was played.**

▶ To learn the **words** to describe what you hear.

Hints

Time signature

▶ Tapping or clapping the rhythm and stressing the strong beats while you listen is perhaps the easiest and most effective way to work out the time signature.

▶ Don't forget that the time might be simple (where the beat is easily divisible by 2) or compound (where the beat is easily divisible by 3).

▶ All of the time signatures for this grade appeared in earlier grades, so you might find it useful to refer to Aural Book 1 which includes more information about time signatures and hints on recognising them.

Hints

Dynamics

> Dynamic changes add interest to music, and the test piece will contain a number of variations of dynamic. Listen first for the overall dynamic plan from phrase to phrase. Then listen for rising and falling within phrases, echo effects and other contrasts. Listen for occasions where different dynamics are used in each hand, for example when a melody in the left hand needs to be brought out.

> Learn the words to describe different dynamics, as well as the terms used to express gradual dynamic changes (for example *crescendo* and *diminuendo*).

Articulation

> The piece may use a mixture of *staccato* and *legato* notes, as well as accents.

> Explain how the articulation is used, referring to any distinctive features of the piece.

> Consider whether the articulation is the same in both hands.

Question 2

What the examiner will do:

Play the piece twice.

What you will be asked to do:

Tell the examiner about two other characteristics of the piece.

What the question is for:

> To develop your skills in **recognising the styles of pieces of music**, and the **compositional devices** they feature.

> To develop your skills in **recognising how the music was played.**

> To learn the **words** to describe what you hear.

Hints

> Remember that you should avoid any references to features already discussed (time signature, dynamics and articulation).

> This question is similar to Question 2 at Grade 6, so you may find it useful to look back at the hints listed for that question.

> At this level the complexity of the music will be more demanding than at Grade 6.

Question 3

What the examiner will do:

▶ State the opening key of the piece and play the key-chord.

▶ Play the first four bars of the piece once.

What you will be asked to do:

Tell the examiner into which key the music has modulated: the subdominant, dominant or relative key.

What the question is for:

▶ To develop your skills in **recognising key changes (modulations)**.

▶ To learn the **words** to describe what you hear.

Hints

▶ Your answer may be given as either the key or the technical name – for example in C major: 'to G major' or 'to the dominant'.

▶ If you want to state the actual modulated key, think of the possible modulated keys as soon as you are told the key of the piece. For example, a piece in C major could modulate to F major (the subdominant), G major (the dominant) or A minor (the relative minor). A piece in A minor could modulate to D minor (the subdominant), E major (the dominant) or C major (the relative major).

Modulations from major keys

▶ See the hints at Grade 6.

Modulations from minor keys

▶ Learn the circle of 5ths for minor keys. Write the minor keys into the circle of 5ths on page 9 if you need to. By now, you will probably have played (or sung) music and scales & arpeggios in most of these keys.

▶ Modulating to a new key is often achieved by playing the dominant 7th chord of that key. This leads straight to the new key.

▶ There are three possible modulations, one to another minor key (subdominant) and the other two to major keys.

▶ A modulation to the dominant feels as if something bright and exciting has happened.

▶ A modulation to the subdominant involves the act of flattening one of the notes, which can make the effect of the modulation feel less assertive.

▶ In a modulation to the relative major, the flattened 7th of the original key becomes the root note of the dominant 7th chord in the new key. Here is an example in A minor:

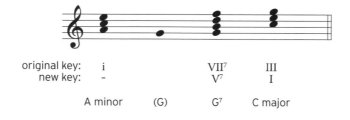

original key:	i		VII⁷	III
new key:	–		V⁷	I
	A minor	(G)	G⁷	C major

Question 4

What the examiner will do:

- Give you a printed copy of the piece.
- Play the piece twice in a version with three changes. The changes may be to the pitch in the melody line or to the rhythm in any part of the piece, or both.

What you will be asked to do:

Identify where the changes were, and whether they were to the pitch or rhythm.

What the question is for:

- To develop your **musical memory.**
- To develop your **awareness of pitch and rhythm.**
- To develop your skills in **relating the music you see to what you hear.**
- To improve the **accuracy of your reading.**

Hints

- You will already have heard the complete original version **four times** before hearing the changed version.
- Remember that **there will not be pitch changes to the bass line.** However, learn to watch both lines carefully for changes in rhythm.
- Either use the printed copy to point to the bar in which each change occurred, or tell the examiner the bar numbers where the changes occurred.
- You do not have to describe the changes; you only need to identify where they occurred and state whether they were to the pitch or to the rhythm.
- Remember that **you are not allowed to make any marks on the copy of the music** you have been given, **or make any other notes during the test.** You could point your finger at the first change to help you remember where it was while you look and listen for the second and third changes.

Try the tests

CD1 11 – 18   Listen to the CD or ask your teacher to play the tests on the piano for you. Each track on the CD contains a complete set of questions. Printed overleaf is the music you will need for Question 4 of each set. Don't look at the music until you reach Question 4. The answers to the tests can be found on pages 15-22 of the **Answer Booklet.**

Music for Grade 7 Question 4

13 Test 3

14 Test 4

15 **Test 5**

16 **Test 6**

17 Test 7

18 Test 8

Grade 8

About the test piece:

metre	$\frac{2}{4}, \frac{3}{4}, \frac{4}{4}, \frac{6}{8}$ or $\frac{5}{8}$
length	12-16 bars
key	major or minor
style	piano style using treble and bass clefs

All questions will be based on the same piece of music.

Question 1

What the examiner will do:

Play the piece once.

What you will be asked to do:

i)   Tell the examiner the **time signature**.
ii) Tell the examiner about the **dynamics**.
iii) Tell the examiner about the **articulation**.

What the question is for:

▶   To learn to recognise the **time signature** of a piece.
▶   To develop your skills in recognising **how the music was played**.
▶   To learn the **words** to describe what you hear.

Hints

Time signature

▶   Tapping or clapping the rhythm and stressing the strong beats while you listen is perhaps the easiest and most effective way to work out the time signature.

▶   Don't forget that the time might be simple (where the beat is easily divisible by 2) or compound (where the beat is easily divisible by 3). See Aural Book 1 for more information on recognising time signatures.

▶   Additionally, at this grade you will need to be able to recognise an irregular time signature – $\frac{5}{8}$. This will usually involve either a 3+2 pattern or a 2+3 pattern, creating an uneven balance between the two halves of the bar. In some cases this gives the effect of a lopsided waltz!

Hints

Dynamics

▶ Dynamic changes add interest to music, and the test piece will contain a number of variations of dynamic. Listen first for the overall dynamic plan from phrase to phrase. Then listen for rising and falling within phrases, echo effects and other contrasts. Listen for occasions where different dynamics are used in each hand, for example when a melody in the left hand needs to be brought out.

▶ Learn the words to describe different dynamics, as well as the terms used to express gradual dynamic changes (for example *crescendo* and *diminuendo*).

Articulation

▶ The piece may use a mixture of *staccato* and *legato* notes, as well as accents.

▶ Explain how the articulation is used, referring to any distinctive features of the piece.

▶ Consider whether the articulation is the same in both hands.

Question 2

What the examiner will do:

Play the piece twice.

What you will be asked to do:

Tell the examiner about three other characteristics of the piece.

What the question is for:

▶ To develop your skills in **recognising the styles of pieces of music**, and the **compositional devices** they feature.

▶ To develop your skills in **recognising how the music was played.**

▶ To learn the **words** to describe what you hear.

Hints

▶ Remember that you should avoid any references to features already discussed (time signature, dynamics and articulation).

▶ This question is similar to Question 2 at Grades 6 and 7, but you are now required to identify three characteristics. You may find it useful to look back at the hints listed for this question at previous grades.

▶ At this level the complexity of the music will be more demanding than at previous grades, and the length of the extracts is increased.

Question 3

What the examiner will do:

▶ Give you a printed copy of the piece.

▶ Play the piece twice in a version with three changes. The changes may be to the pitch or to the rhythm, or both.

What you will be asked to do:

Identify where the changes were, and whether they were to the pitch or rhythm.

What the question is for:

▶ To develop your **musical memory.**

▶ To develop your **awareness of pitch and rhythm.**

▶ To develop your skills in **relating the music you see to what you hear.**

▶ To improve the **accuracy of your reading.**

Hints

▶ You will already have heard the complete original version **three** times before hearing the changed version.

▶ So far you have only had to identify pitch changes in the melody at the top of the texture and in the treble clef. At this grade changes of pitch might occur in the bass clef or inner parts too.

▶ Make sure you are familiar with music in the bass clef as well as music using two clefs (most piano music).

▶ Either use the printed copy to point to the bar in which each change occurred, or tell the examiner the bar numbers where the changes occurred.

▶ You do not have to describe the changes; you only need to identify where they occurred and state whether they were to the pitch or to the rhythm.

▶ Remember that **you are not allowed to make any marks on the copy of the music** you have been given, **or make any other notes during the test.** You could point your finger at the first change to help you remember where it was while you look and listen for the second and third changes.

Try the tests

CD2 01 - 07   Listen to the CD or ask your teacher to play the tests on the piano for you. Each track on the CD contains a complete set of questions. Printed opposite is the music you will need for Question 3 of each set. Don't look at the music until you reach Question 3. The answers to the tests can be found on pages 24-37 of the **Answer Booklet.**

Music for Grade 8 Question 3

01 Test 1

02 **Test 2**

03 Test 3

04 **Test 4**

05 Test 5

06 Test 6

07 Test 7

Information for teachers

Instrumentation

In the exam the tests will be played on the piano. In lessons they may be played live or delivered using the CD. Teachers should note that most tests need to be played on the piano owing to the integral nature of harmony and texture at these grades.

Significant features of the test piece

The first two questions asked at each grade are concerned with exploring candidates' perception of the characteristics of the piece and the performance.

The first question focuses on three compositional elements of the test piece: time signature, dynamics and articulation.

The second question is less specific, allowing candidates to bring their own perceptual skills into play and to develop their own approach to listening and understanding. 'Characteristics' allows candidates to comment on any noteworthy aspects of the piece apart from those discussed in the first question. These may include styles (which in many cases will relate to period), features commonly associated with those styles (for example Alberti bass in Classical style music, swung quavers in jazz), dance forms (for example minuet, sicilienne), texture (melody and chordal accompaniment, two-part counterpoint, etc) or compositional devices (such as ostinato, imitation, melodic sequence, melody moving to the bass, etc).

The styles of music are widely varied, and listening and discussion based on a wide range of pieces will provide good preparation for this section of the test.

Students who are unfamiliar with the sound of the piano will need to experience how differing articulations, textures and dynamics will sound, and should note that contrast in some or all of these elements is built into each test.

Perception of pitch tonality and key relationship

In Grades 6 and 7 candidates are asked to identify modulations. This builds on the perception of tonality explored from Grade 3 onwards. Modulations occur halfway through the test piece, and may be to the subdominant, dominant or relative key. At Grade 6 all the test pieces are in major keys, while at Grade 7 they may be in either major or minor keys.

Candidates may alternatively give their answers as key names.

Perception of change

Candidates will be asked questions relating to changes made by the examiner to the test piece, which by this stage in the test will have been heard a number of times. In each case candidates are shown a copy of the test piece and asked to locate and explain changes made to it in subsequent playings. This question develops reading skills and ear-to-eye links, as well as musical memory (of pitch and rhythm) over an increasing timescale and in a widening variety of musical contexts.

The demands of this question increase in a carefully structured way, beginning in Grade 6 with two changes to the melody line, which may be to the pitch or rhythm or both. In Grade 7 there are three changes to find; pitch changes will again be confined to the melody line, although the entire texture is now under scrutiny for changes to the rhythm. In Grade 8 changes of pitch are no longer confined to the melody line, and both types of change may therefore occur in any part of the texture.

Marking

In all exams the aural tests are worth 10% of the total marks available. Marks for the aural tests are awarded holistically; that is without a fixed number of marks being allotted to each question. This enables examiners to indicate not only whether answers were correct, but also to give due credit to promptness and confidence of response. In general, all questions should be regarded as equally important in terms of marking.

Full assessment criteria are available from Trinity's website www.trinitycollege.com

Track listing

CD 1

Grade	Test	Track no.
Grade 6	1	01
	2	02
	3	03
	4	04
	5	05
	6	06
	7	07
	8	08
	9	09
	10	10
Grade 7	1	11
	2	12
	3	13
	4	14
	5	15
	6	16
	7	17
	8	18

CD 2

Grade	Test	Track no.
Grade 8	1	01
	2	02
	3	03
	4	04
	5	05
	6	06
	7	07

Produced and engineered by Ken Blair
Recorded at Red Gables Studio

Piano: Peter Wild
Voiceover: Luise Horrocks